This book belongs to

**Alissa Sadler**

Written by the
Reading Initiative Committee
of The Texas Speech-Language
Hearing Association.

## AUTHORS

Cynthia Campbell          Martha McGlothlin
Terri C. Haynes           Julie Noel
Elena Jaramillo           Ann Shaw King
Judith P. Keller          Martha Wristen
Carolyn McCall

## Dedicated to all the children of Texas who are learning how to read.

# Matt Learns to Read

## ILLUSTRATED BY KEEVA ANDERSON

TEXAS SPEECH-LANGUAGE-HEARING ASSOCIATION

Designed by:

Vickie Raines Spurgin
The Raines Design Group, McKinney Texas

ISBN 0-9674783-0-8

©1998 **Texas Speech-Language Hearing Association**

2nd printing, September, 1999

**TEXAS SPEECH-LANGUAGE-HEARING ASSOCIATION**
8317 Cross Park, Suite 150 · Austin, Texas 78754
1-888-SAY-TSHA (729-8742) · www.txsha.com

Once upon a time, in the great state
of Texas, there was a little boy named
Matt who didn't know how to read.

"I'm going to school today," said Matt.
"So I can learn to read."

Matt had a friend named Rosa. She was older and already knew how to read. "Hi, Matt. Are you ready for school?" asked Rosa.

On the way to school,
Matt and Rosa walked
by Mrs. Keller's house.

"Hi, Mrs. Keller. I'm going to school
today so I can learn to read," said Matt.

"Good for you, Matt!" said Mrs. Keller.

"I already know how to read," said Rosa.
"See that sign. It says HOUSE FOR SALE."

Matt listened to what Rosa had said and he looked at the yard sign with the circles and dashes and squiggly lines and he tried really hard to read. "House for Sale," repeated Matt.

Matt and Rosa saw their neighbor, Mr. Williams, in the park. He was jogging and pushing a baby stroller.

"Hi, Mr. Williams," said Matt. "I'm going to school today so I can learn to read."

"Good luck, puffed Mr. Williams.

"I already know how to read," bragged Rosa.
"See that sign. It says WET PAINT."

Matt looked at the wet sign with the circles and dashes and squiggly lines and he tried really hard to read. "WET PAINT," repeated Matt.

Matt and Rosa walked by Joe's Fruit and Vegetable Stand. "Hi Joe," said Matt. "I'm going to school today, so I can learn to read."

You're really growing up!" Joe said as he waved.

"I already know how to read," said Rosa.
"See that sign. It says PEACHES."

Matt looked at the big sign with the circles and
dashes and squiggly lines and he tried really hard
to read. "Peaches," repeated Matt.

Matt and Rosa stopped at the corner.
They looked both ways and saw Officer Jane.
"Hi, Officer Jane," said Matt. "I'm going to
school today, so I can learn to read."

"Reading is very important,"
Officer Jane answered.

"I already know how to read.
See Officer Jane's car. It says CALL 911
EMERGENCY," said Rosa.

Matt looked at the blue car sign with the circles and
dashes and squiggly lines and he tried really hard
to read. "Call 911 Emergency." repeated Matt.

Matt and Rosa saw Sam opening his store. "Hi, Sam. I'm going to school today, so I can learn to read," said Matt.

"Great! Then you can help me in the store!" Sam replied.

Rosa pointed to the sign and said, "I already know how to read. See that sign. It says CLOSED."

Matt looked at the door sign with the circles and dashes and squiggly lines. He tried really hard to read. "Closed." repeated Matt.

TACOS

FRESH

Help Wanted

CLOSED
cerrado

I

When they finally got to the school, they saw Mrs. Lee helping children cross the street.

"Hi, Mrs. Lee," said Matt. "I'm going to school, so I can learn to read."

"I already know how to read, Mrs. Lee!
See your sign. It says STOP," said Rosa.

Matt looked at the bright, red sign with the circles and dashes and squiggly lines and he tried really hard to read. "Stop," repeated Matt.

Matt and Rosa saw Mrs. Garcia, the school principal.

"Good morning, Matt and Rosa. Are you ready for your first day of school? asked Mrs. Garcia.

"I am," said Rosa.

Matt nodded yes.

"Matt, are you ready to learn to read?"
asked Mrs. Garcia.

# DEAR FAMILIES,

On behalf of the Texas Speech-Language-Hearing Association, we would like your help in one of the most important projects we've ever undertaken—helping young children learn to read. We all know the important role that reading plays in school and in life. We are now finding that the single most important activity for laying the foundation for literacy and learning to read is reading aloud to children, especially during the pre-school years.

Reading begins in your home as you play the role of your child's first and most important teacher. While having fun as you read to your child, you are "teaching" the basic concepts your child needs in order to understand people, objects, events, thoughts, and feelings. You are also helping develop the language and literacy skills your child needs in order to express these concepts. Included in this booklet you will find some helpful hints for choosing books for children and for reading aloud to children.

While reading aloud from your child's favorite storybook is a wonderful way to spend quality time together and to lay the foundation for language, literacy, and reading, there are a number of other ways you may help your child. You're helping your child when you:

- talk with your child and share stories, ideas, and information through conversation
- let your child see and hear you read and follow directions
- write the words for a picture your child draws
- ask your child to help you make lists and/or keep records
- read a note, memo, or letter you are writing to your child
- let your child see you reading for pleasure and/or business
- point out to your child that you are reading the ingredients or contents of a package or a container
- read signs to your child
- share greeting cards with your child

As you can see, there are many opportunities, throughout the day, for reading to your child. Take advantage of these opportunities and help your child get a head start on learning to read.

# Choosing Books for Children

■ **Birth to One Year**
- Durable, "chew-proof" books made of cardboard or cloth with clear, colorful, realistic pictures
- Books of nursery rhymes

■ **One to Three Years**
- Board and cloth books with pictures toddlers can name
- Mother Goose books
- Books that contain "fun-sounding" words and sentences
- Books that contain words and sentences that are repeated over and over
- Books about familiar people and things such as families, babies, animals, toys, food
- Books that ask children to do something such as "Pat the bunny"

■ **Three to Five Years**
- Predictable books such as "Brown Bear, Brown Bear"
- Books that contain rhythm and rhyme
- Books that encourage children to have fun playing with words and sounds
- Books that contain a simple storyline or plot
- Books that contain a small amount of print per page; more space devoted to pictures
- Books that focus on children's interests
- Books that are appropriate for the children's vocabulary
- Books that contain pictures that are clear, colorful, and realistic
- Books that you, the reader, will enjoy as well
- Story length that matches children's attention spans

■ **Primary School-Age**
- Books that contain bright, realistic pictures
- Books that contain more print per page than before
- Books that contain plots that are more involved
- Books about less familiar people and things, such as astronauts, children from foreign lands, experiences they've never had
- Story length that matches children's attention spans

# TIPS FOR READING ALOUD TO CHILDREN

■ *Begin reading to your child soon after he/she is born.*
Remember, children are never too young to spend time with books and have someone read to them, or tell them stories about pictures on a page.

■ *Set aside a special read-aloud time each day.*
Just before naptime and/or bedtime seem to be especially good times for reading aloud. Young children enjoy "reading" and splashing in the tub with plastic or vinyl books.

■ *Remember to make read-aloud time a "snuggle" time*
Snuggling together as you share a book with a child is important in many ways.

■ *Have a variety of books available for your child.*
- Remember to include non-fiction books as your child gets older.
- Choose books about topics your child may be curious about such as "how" or why" things happen.
- Consider making your own "books" by using photographs, pictures cut from magazines, or pictures you and/or your child draw.

■ *Choose good books.*
- Begin by choosing wordless books, picture books, and books of nursery rhymes.
- Make sure the vocabulary and the content are appropriate for your child's interest, vocabulary, and level of comprehension.
- Make sure the pictures are clear and realistic and correspond to the words on the page. You may tell the story by talking about the pictures.
- Select books for your child that are about familiar events and experiences that might occur in his/her own life.
- Choose books with content that is unbiased in terms of gender, race, culture, age, individual differences, and individual abilities.

- Select books that you enjoy as well. Remember, much of your child's enjoyment of books is the result of knowing that you're also enjoying the book.
- Select a variety of books, and let your child help select books whenever possible.
- Look for books that have repetitive language, rhythm, or rhymes that your child can say with you or plots in which your child can predict what will happen next.
- Ask the librarian at your local library for suggestions of books and/or ask other parents about the books their children enjoy.

■ *Familiarize yourself with each book before reading it to your child.*
Remember, the more familiar you are with the story, the easier it will be for you to interpret the story and to ask meaningful questions about it, such as "What do you think will happen next?"

■ *Introduce each book to your child.*
Read the title of the book out loud, then look at and talk about the pictures on the cover. Invite your child to guess what the book will be about. Tell your child who wrote the book and who drew/painted the pictures. When appropriate, familiarize your child with the book's author and illustrator by telling him/her the name of each.

■ *Try to match reading time to your child's attention span and comfort level.*
If your child becomes restless before the story is finished, you might say, "I like this story, but it's a little long. Let's finish it tomorrow."

■ *Ask questions that have more than one answer.*

  ■ Ask questions that will encourage your child to think and talk.
    - "What do you think might happen if…?"
    - "How might the story have ended differently?"

  ■ Ask questions that will encourage your child to give his/her opinion.
    - "What was your favorite part of the story?"
    - "Would you like to have (name of a character) as a friend?" "Why or why not?"
    - "Did you enjoy this book?" "Why or why not?"

- *Remember that your child's interests in and preferences for certain types of books will change with age and development.*

  Infants simply enjoy being read to, hearing the sound of your voice, and having you near. Toddlers enjoy board books, big books, and books that have few words on each page with pictures that are clear and easily identified.

- *Read familiar favorites over and over.*

  As your child becomes more familiar with a book, he/she will begin to "read" it with you. Your child will learn to recognize certain words and phrases and will repeat them with you.

- *Remind your child,*

# " BE NICE
# TO YOUR BOOKS,
# THEY ARE
# YOUR FRIENDS. "